dream
travel

dream
travel

jenni davis

Publication in this form copyright © Jarrold Publishing 2005

Text copyright © Jarrold Publishing

The moral right of the author has been asserted

Series editor Jenni Davis

Designed by Mark Buckingham

Pictures researched by Jenni Davis

A CIP catalogue for this book is available from the British Library.

Published by:
Jarrold Publishing
Healey House, Dene Road, Andover, Hampshire, SP10 2AA
www.britguides.com

Set in Gill Sans Light

Printed in Singapore

ISBN 1 84165 156 7   1/05

Pitkin is an imprint of Jarrold Publishing, Norwich

contents

introduction

For the early explorer, a compass was essential (this one was made in 1617 by Elias Allen). For the dream traveller, a porter to carry the luggage (left) was far more important!

There is nothing like an endless traffic jam or a long airport delay to evoke nostalgia for a time when travelling for pleasure was a completely new and thrilling phenomenon, a real adventure with all the heady excitement that this magical word conjures up.

The places that we now take so much for granted were once considered very exotic – France, Italy, Egypt. In the 18th century, a visit to these countries entailed endless hours of planning – the transport, the route, where to stay, what to wear, finding a guide who understood the delights and pitfalls of foreign travel ….

Gradually, new methods of transport opened up the world still further, and the intrepid could visit America on an ocean liner or cross Russia by train. And eventually, inevitably, an entrepreneur – Thomas Cook – hit on the idea of organized 'tourism'. By the turn of the 19th century, dream travel was at its dreamiest height.

the world opens up

TRAVEL ISN'T A NEW IDEA, OF COURSE — PEOPLE HAVE BEEN MOVING BETWEEN COUNTRIES AND CROSSING SEAS FOR HUNDREDS OF CENTURIES. BUT THEIR PURPOSE, USUALLY, WAS NOT TO ENHANCE THEIR KNOWLEDGE OR TO TAKE A HOLIDAY — IT WAS TO FIGHT WARS AND CONQUER OTHER LANDS.

However, when the Italian-born sailor Christopher Columbus, under the patronage of Ferdinand and Isabella of Castile, discovered the New World in the late 15th century, he inspired journeys with a new aim in mind, which would take root and flourish in the years ahead. The aim was exploration.

Within a hundred years, a number of English adventurers followed Columbus's example and headed west, both to explore and to try to end the Spanish monopoly of America. Sir Walter Raleigh established Virginia, the first English settlement in the Americas; Sir Francis Drake became the first Englishman to circumnavigate the world; Sir Martin Frobisher attempted to find a route to China via the Northwest Passage around Canada.

These tales sound wonderfully romantic, especially associated as they are with the outstanding reign of Elizabeth I – 'Gloriana'. In reality it was anything but romantic; many explorers died at sea, lost in storms or defeated in battle or succumbing to illness. Dream travel was yet to come.

Christopher Columbus prepares to set sail on his first voyage of discovery in 1492 aboard the Santa Maria. Sir Walter Raleigh founded the colony of Virginia (above) in 1585.

A miniature of an 18th-century colonist relaxing on a terrace in India with his attendants at hand.

By the time another great queen, Victoria, came to the throne in 1837, there had been some extraordinary changes in the world.

In 1620 the Puritan Pilgrim Fathers had left England on board the *Mayflower* and sailed to America, where they set up home in their newly created colony of Plymouth, Massachusetts – the first of countless English emigrants to settle the New World. In 1699 the Chinese port of Canton had been opened to traders of the East India Company, and trade with China had increased during the following century. Singapore was acquired for Britain and colonized in 1824, and the island of Hong Kong in 1841.

The landing of the Pilgrim Fathers at Plymouth, Massachusetts on 11 December 1620, under the watchful eye of a Native American.

Between 1743 and 1767 Robert Clive had conquered much of India and established British supremacy there, earning him the title 'Clive of India'. The English explorer Captain James Cook had sailed to the Antipodes and in 1770 claimed the east coast of Australia for Britain; as yet its main claim to fame was as a penal colony, a far-flung place where convicts could be deported and conveniently forgotten. The British Empire had blossomed, but hardship was still the name of the travelling game.

It took a revolution to get dream travel well and truly under way – the Industrial Revolution.

Brunel's Great Eastern, launched c.1857, had accommodation for 4,000 passengers.

Richard Trevithick's locomotive engine runs around a circular railroad in London's Euston Square in 1808.

In 1712, a Devonshire blacksmith, Thomas Newcomen, invented the steam engine to pump water out of coal mines. It was an unsophisticated but effective piece of machinery, if somewhat uneconomical to run, and it spawned all future steam engines. It was 50 years before Newcomen's basic design was modified by James Watt to make it more efficient, and still longer before one Richard Trevithick, a Cornish mining engineer, harnessed steam power to create forward motion.

In 1808 a locomotive engine built by Trevithick chugged around on a 100-feet (30-metre) radius circular railroad in London at the daringly high speed of 10 miles (16km) an hour, pulling passengers in an open carriage. George Stephenson developed the idea and in 1825 his steam locomotive *Locomotion* hauled the inaugural Stockton & Darlington Railway train. Timothy Hackworth followed suit with his engine *Royal George*, inspiring investment in railways and starting Britain's railway export business. By the 1840s, railways were very definitely the way to travel.

Steam was also replacing sail as the means of powering ships. Steam ferries plied rivers and crossed the English Channel from 1812, and in 1838 Brunel's steamship *Great Western* docked in New York.

Soon there would be elegant passenger liners, and trains resembling luxury hotels on wheels. The golden age of dream travel had at last begun.

*This advertisement for
the new magazine
The Traveller appeared
in the* Illustrated
London News *in 1900.*

*A laden carriage of
Thomas Cook tourists
taking a guided trip
around Paris.*

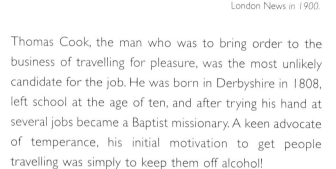

Thomas Cook, the man who was to bring order to the business of travelling for pleasure, was the most unlikely candidate for the job. He was born in Derbyshire in 1808, left school at the age of ten, and after trying his hand at several jobs became a Baptist missionary. A keen advocate of temperance, his initial motivation to get people travelling was simply to keep them off alcohol!

His first organized 'tour', in July 1841, was a day's outing from Leicester to Loughborough enjoyed by 570 members of temperance groups; ten years later, he brought 165,000 people to London from all over Britain by train to visit the Great Exhibition in the Crystal Palace. Every aspect of the trip was arranged by Cook, from transport to lodgings and meals; the package tour was born, and tourism was now officially an industry.

In the intervening years, Cook had taken hordes of grateful working-class trippers on holidays to British seaside resorts and spa towns, but a trip to the Paris Exhibition in 1855 inspired him to venture further afield with a more affluent clientele. The following year he escorted a group of tourists on a railway tour of Europe and in the early 1860s opened the first travel agency, Thomas Cook and Sons.

THE TRAVELLER

FOR·WHOM·THE·WORLD·IS·A·PLAYGROUND·

THIS Journal is on sale not only all over the United Kingdom, but also *in every Travel and Tourist Centre throughout the World, through the Depots and Agencies of*

MESSRS. THOMAS COOK AND SON.

Thus **THE TRAVELLER** may be bought in Lucerne, Rome, Venice, Norway, the Tyrol, &c., &c.— in short, wherever English-speaking Tourists foregather.

PRICE SIXPENCE.
NUMBER ONE NOW READY.

A High-Class Illustrated Sixpenny Weekly Journal, finely printed on Art paper, profusely illustrated, and appealing at all seasons to all classes who travel and tour for health, business, or pleasure.

THERE IS NO SIMILAR PAPER PUBLISHED IN ANY COUNTRY.

The scheme of **THE TRAVELLER** is entirely novel, and the system of circulation and distribution equally so.

FEATURES:

Travel Notes and News from our own Correspondents in all the Tourist Centres.

Motor - Car, Yachting, Photographic, Guide-Book, Passport and Money, and other Notes and News.

Passengers disembark from Thomas Cook's Nile steamer Masr to be taken by mule to see the sights.

The enterprise was a huge success. Within a very short time, branches of the Thomas Cook travel agency were to be found everywhere in Europe and business was booming. Cook representatives, clad in the company's distinctive livery, appeared on every railway station and hotels were built to accommodate the enthusiastic new breed of travellers.

In 1869 the Suez Canal was opened to provide a direct shipping route to the Far East, and suddenly there was an

intriguing new destination craze – Egypt. The Prince and Princess of Wales (later King Edward VII and Queen Alexandra) were pleasure-seekers extraordinaire, their glamorous lifestyle emulated by many, and when they headed south to open the canal, Cook followed in their wake with a group of keen tourists. Needless to say, a

leisurely trip up the Nile was the highlight of a visit to Egypt – at one time, the Thomas Cook organization owned every steamer that plied the river. The Nile journey ended in Cairo, where Cook was proprietor of the opulent Shepheard's Hotel.

Thomas Cook certainly made life easy for late 19th-century tourists, but the locations for his 'grand tour' had been mapped out well over a hundred years earlier by countless young British gentlemen with a thirst for knowledge.

This illustration of Cook's Nile steamer Egypt appeared in a German magazine in 1909.

the grand tour

A view of the Pantheon in Rome, with the statue of the mythical hero Hercules in the foreground. An elegant young aristocrat (above) poses against a background of the Amphitheatre of Taormina in Rome.

THE 1700S SUCCESSFULLY SHRUGGED OFF THE TRAUMAS AND DISASTERS OF THE PREVIOUS CENTURY — RELIGIOUS TURMOIL, THE CIVIL WAR, THE SHIFT OF SOVEREIGNTY FROM MONARCH TOWARDS PARLIAMENT, A FEARFUL OUTBREAK OF BUBONIC PLAGUE, THE DEVASTATING GREAT FIRE OF LONDON — AND MOVED FORWARD INTO A NEW AGE OF CIVILIZATION, GENTILITY AND GRACIOUS LIVING.

Wars rumbled away in Europe and America throughout the 18th century, but the problems they caused were offset by a rapidly increasing wealth created by trade with the growing colonies and an unprecedented level of productivity in Britain. The aristocracy was rich and powerful, and spent enormous sums of money building sumptuous mansions at the heart of huge estates. Classical style was favoured for architecture and decoration, and genteel manners were essential for the families who lived in these stately homes.

The best way for the young up-and-coming British aristocrats to acquire their classical knowledge and European polish was at first hand, and thus the custom of the Grand Tour was conceived. Until the violent French Revolution made travel through that country temporarily ill advised for the privileged, many young men headed south, chaperoned by a tutor, to broaden their intellectual, artistic and social horizons.

The groves of the Baths of Apollo in the gardens of Versailles, painted in 1713.

A stagecoach piled with luggage was the mode of transport for any 18th-century traveller without his own carriage.

The Grand Tour was of necessity a long, leisurely affair, lasting as many as three or four years. The destination was Italy, where the young gentlemen, who had recently completed their formal education, could witness their studies in history and the classics spring to life and take on real meaning in their proper context. The typical itinerary passed through France and Switzerland, to emerge in northern Italy and carry on southwards.

The Tour began with a Channel crossing on a packet boat, and progressed from Calais in a horse-drawn carriage. The journey from Calais to Paris took a week, but as the traveller visited en route the pretty medieval towns of Normandy and Brittany, with their abbeys and cathedrals, it was a week well spent.

Paris at that time was not quite the irresistibly chic, cultural city it is today – indeed, it was noisy, over-populated and filthy. But the bridges of the Seine were there to be admired, as were the Champs Elysées and the Tuileries, Luxembourg and Palais Royal gardens; and an outing to the Palace of Versailles, the court of the king and queen, was a must for the aristocrat who aspired to a touch of that desirable French etiquette.

Joseph Wright of Derby
brought an air of
romance to Italian
bandits, shown here
lurking in a grotto.

The thrill of taking the Grand Tour was tempered by the extreme terrors of travelling. The tutors who accompanied the young tourists were also expected to protect them; since these tutors were often meek and obliging clergymen, presumably they relied heavily upon divine protection!

A dramatic performance
before a packed house
at Milan's Teatro alla
Scala opera house.

The route from Paris down to Italy presented two alternatives, each with its own pitfalls. Most favoured making the journey through Switzerland before crossing the Alps into Italy; but those who found the prospect of the hazardous Alpine route simply too alarming headed for the Côte d'Azur and the coast road. This was hardly an improvement, as the Mediterranean towns were yet to become fashionable, and the road was a notorious spot for bandits.

One way or another Italy was reached, and tourists headed for the first stop, Milan, where they admired the art and, towards the end of the century, attended the opera at Teatro alla Scala. From there they continued to Vicenza, Verona and Padua; it was not uncommon for the young men to further their education at Padua's famous university. They then took their courage in both hands and set off for the delights and dangers of Venice.

A view of the Palace of St Mark by Canaletto, the definitive painter of 18th-century Venetian scenes.

Masked figures merge into the gloom of a Venetian coffee house. Costumed and masked balls were a feature of Venetian social life..

Robbery, kidnap, murder and a dire assault on the nostrils were just some of the horrors of Venice; fortunately, they were more than offset by the palatial architecture, the churches and monuments, and most of all the marvellous spectacle of the processions and pageantry of the doges (the city's chief magistrates), now long gone. Life here was flamboyant, colourful and unique; the wonderful sight of the Great Doge sailing down the Grand Canal, with a flotilla of smaller ships in his wake manned by liveried gondoliers, would have lingered in the memory long after the stench of garbage was forgotten.

By contrast, the pleasures of Florence were strictly intellectual and high spirits were quenched by an atmosphere of quiet respect for the priceless treasures. The city was both safe and solemn, the home of the Renaissance masters and of their patrons, the Medici family. Michelangelo's *David* stood outside the Palazzo Vecchio, and Giotto's bell tower pierced the skyline, as it does today.

The next stop on the itinerary was Rome, the land of Julius Caesar, a name familiar to every schoolboy. Here the traveller stepped far back to the time of the ancient city, when the tentacles of the great empire spread far and wide.

The volcanic Mount Vesuvius erupts beneath a silvery moonlit sky.

A romantic portrayal of architectural ruins by Charles Louis Clerisseau.

There was a marked British presence in 18th-century Rome, testimony to the keen interest of the Grand Tourist. There was plenty to fascinate – the dazzling palaces of the equally dazzling Italian aristocracy, the pageantry surrounding the Pope and of course the remnants of the city's history. At that time, the remnants needed a certain flight of imagination to bring them to life, as the ancient sites were in a poor state and mainly housed animals and young girls of questionable virtue whose presence drowned out the echoes of the past.

From cultural Rome, it was south to Naples, which in the 18th century was the biggest city in Italy and the most vibrant, ruled by the dynamic, glamorous Bourbons. Here was a novel attraction – to climb up to the surrounding hills and look down on the bay and its dramatic volcanoes, particularly at night when the fire reflected on the water.

Towards the end of the century, excavations began at the ancient cities of Herculaneum and Pompeii, buried almost two thousand years earlier beneath a river of molten lava from Mount Vesuvius. To be here at this time to witness the cities emerging like the phoenix from the ashes must have made a truly memorable climax to the Grand Tour.

A portrait of the Grand Tourist William Perry, with the Colosseum as a background.

William Wendell proudly displays his treasures at Newby Hall, Yorkshire (above); the Italian sculptor Antonio Canova poses (right) with Henry Tresham and a plaster model for his statue of Cupid and Psyche.

Then, as now, part of the fun was to return home with a visual record of your travels and a few souvenirs to display around the house. The difference is that now we would take endless photographs, and perhaps buy a piece of local pottery or a little watercolour as a keepsake; for the 18th-century traveller, the only option was to engage an artist to paint you against a suitably impressive background (the Italian painter Pompeo Girolamo Battoni did a roaring trade in portraits during the peak years of the Grand Tour), and souvenirs were often genuine artefacts that were worth a fortune and had to be shipped home with infinite care.

It is these curios and works of art that today form a major part of the artistic treasures on display in the nation's stately homes. Paintings were a favourite acquisition, and when the excavation of the ancient sites began in earnest in the late 18th century, British collectors flocked to add statuary and sculpture, mouldings and urns to their collections.

Monuments in the classical style of Italian and Greek temples and pavilions began to appear in newly landscaped gardens such as Stowe and Stourhead, memories of the sunlit days of the Grand Tour recreated beneath bleaker English skies.

dream travelling

FOR TRAVEL TO BE REALLY DREAMY, THE MEANS OF TRANSPORT MUST BE EVERY BIT AS FABULOUS AS THE DESTINATION. WHEN THE GOLDEN AGE OF TRAVELLING DAWNED IN THE LATE 19TH CENTURY, EVERYTHING WAS IN PLACE FOR STYLISH, LUXURIOUS, TRULY ENVIABLE TRAVEL.

Gone were the days of crossing Europe at a snail's pace in a draughty horse-drawn carriage. Now, endless miles of railway track had been laid and tunnels blasted through mountains, overcoming seemingly impossible obstacles. Trains had progressed from cramped carriages with rows of uncomfortably hard benches to warm, welcoming individual sleeping compartments, the innovation of a forward-thinking American, George Pullman.

A train in the snow, painted by the Impressionist artist Monet in 1875; Cunard's steamship Scotia (above) depicted by Toulouse-Lautrec.

Sea voyages were no longer made aboard uncomfortable utilitarian ships; the new passenger liners and cruise ships, operated by Cunard, White Star and P&O (names that shriek high living), were a small piece of heaven. Even so, to be really chic one had to travel in a cabin that was port-side out and starboard home, the origin of the word 'posh'.

The 20th century brought two new means of travelling – the aeroplane and the automobile. Suddenly, journeys that had once taken weeks could be completed in hours, bringing both comfort and convenience but perhaps heralding the end of leisurely dream travel.

A Pullman car of the European Compagnie Internationale des Wagons Lits (CIWL).

Queen Victoria, Prince Albert and their children board the Royal Train, c.1850. A poster for the Trans-Siberian Railway (right).

George Pullman – 'inventor, improver and businessman' – transformed the railway carriage from a rudimentary hut on wheels into an elegant, wood-panelled compartment with seats that folded into beds. At night, a solicitous porter made up the beds, lit the lamps and poured hot water into the hand basin for washing. Later, dining cars were added, a distinct improvement on picnicking or the frantic scrum for the station buffet.

A young man from a Belgian banking family, Georges Nagelmackers, took the best ideas of George Pullman and brought them to Europe, where he founded the Compagnie Internationale des Wagons Lits (CIWL). The Pullman Company was later brought to Britain, where one of its triumphs was *The Golden Arrow* service – an attractive confection painted in brown and cream and handsomely decorated with art deco marquetry – that ran from London to Dover. After the Channel crossing, an identical train, the *Flèche d'Or*, completed the journey to Paris.

However, in spite of the competition from Pullman, the CIWL dominated Europe and even spread as far as China via the steppes of Russia – the Trans-Siberian railway covered 4,700 miles (7,500kms) from Moscow to Vladivostok and the journey lasted several very monotonous weeks.

A poster c.1930
advertising the Simplon
Orient Express.

The Orient Express
near Constantinople, its
journey's end; passengers
enjoy the stylish dining
car in an illustration of
1884 (right).

A name that conjures up all the best elements of travelling for pleasure – romance, style, glamour, decadence – is the *Orient Express*, the invention of Georges Nagelmackers. This delectable train was the ultimate in travel comfort – the sheets were silk and the blankets pure wool, and on the dining tables were crisp linen, monogrammed porcelain and Baccarat crystal. The shared bathroom was scented and luxurious, the ladies' salon feminine and pretty in contrast to the gentlemen's salon with its masculine leather club chairs. Everywhere was thick carpeting and low lighting, soft velvet and rich, heavy damask.

The *Orient Express*, which made its maiden trip in 1883, ran from glitzy Paris to Constantinople in mysterious, oriental Istanbul; but most travellers opted to take a curtailed trip and enjoy the culture in the Austrian city of Vienna.

The train and its passengers were an irresistible source of inspiration for writers, perhaps most famously Agatha Christie's crime novel *Murder on the Orient Express*, in which there is a very unusual twist!

The P&O passenger liner Strathhaven, *built in 1931, with its distinctive white livery.*

The cabin lounge on the promenade deck of the P&O ship Queen Mary, *from a souvenir brochure of 1935.*

For many years – because the journey was slow, tortuous and often dangerous – travelling by ship was something considered only by those desperate to leave their homeland and begin a new life in the colonies, by devil-may-care adventurers or by civil servants posted to far-flung corners of the British Empire. But steam power opened up new possibilities and the squalor of the 'steerage' area was offset by the splendor of first-class travel.

Two of the three big names – Cunard and P&O – began as mail shipping companies. Cunard headed to North America; P&O first to the Iberian Peninsula and then to Egypt, India, Singapore, Hong Kong and Australia as the Empire grew. The third, White Star, originally served Australia with traditional sailing vessels during the gold rush. Over time, each company diversified and eventually built liners and cruise ships designed specifically for transporting passengers.

P&O is said to have invented the concept of cruising (the novelist Thackeray records taking a 'delightful Mediterranean cruise' in 1844, albeit on a series of ships), and by 1904 the company had joined forces with Thomas Cook's organization to combine cruising with shore excursions. The cruising craze really took off between the World Wars, with P&O at the helm both metaphorically and literally.

*A floating playground –
passengers on board a
liner set off to pass the
time with a deck game.*

The most luxurious
ship of its time, the
SS Titanic was doomed
never to complete its
maiden voyage.

The world's first super-liner, the *Oceanic*, was built by the White Star Line (the names of all their ships ended in 'ic'). The company's motto was 'comfort, rather than speed', partly because their shipbuilders hadn't the technology to build for speed! Speed was the province of the Cunard Line, whose ships won the prestigious Blue Riband for the fastest transatlantic crossing.

It was White Star's need to maintain a competitive edge that led to the building of their fabulously opulent but ill-fated *Titanic*, which hit an iceberg and sank on its maiden voyage, with severe loss of life. One survivor recalled that the band kept on playing as the passengers scrambled for the lifeboats.

As long as the weather was clement and the sea calm (seasickness being undignified as well as unpleasant), life on board ship was never dull. The crossing began with a bon-voyage party for friends, and every day there were cocktails, dining and dancing; a regular promenade around the deck was desirable, both for exercise and for keeping a high profile among influential passengers – and there was always the promise of a little shipboard romance.

'If you are ever shipwrecked, my dearest Laura – do contrive to get the catastrophe conducted by the Peninsula and Oriental Company. I believe other companies drown you ...'

Letter from Mrs Dulcimer to her friend Laura, 1863

Fashionable ladies pose elegantly on the Casino Terrace at the resort of Juan-les-Pin, Côte d'Azur.

An Imperial Airways poster with the message of the 1920s, 'Move with the times'. The first cross-Channel passenger flight, 17 August 1910 (right).

In 1899, a determined American, Wilbur Wright, said, 'I am convinced that human flight is both possible and practical.' Of course, he meant not literally but by aeroplane, and he and his brother Orville went on to prove the point, building on the research of earlier would-be aviation inventors to fly the first successful heavier-than-air machine in 1903. By 1909 they had patented their flying machine and formed an aircraft production company.

In Britain, civil aviation began in earnest after the First World War and the British air travel industry was born, albeit dependent on good weather and a somewhat dubious navigation system.

In 1924, the nation's first state airline was formed – Imperial Airways Ltd. Now you could fly to France, Belgium, Germany and Switzerland and – as the name implies – to outposts of the British Empire. Suddenly it was possible to pop over to the chic resorts of northern France or head down to the Mediterranean where hotels and restaurants and casinos lined up in the sunshine to take the stressful edge off a rapidly changing environment. Life for the dream traveller took on a thrilling new dimension as the wide world began its inexorable process of shrinkage.

 dream travelling

*An automobile arrives
in London's Belgravia
in this illustration from
John Strickland Goodall's
An Edwardian Season.*

*Frank Salisbury's painting
The Enchanted Road,
c.1928, demonstrates
the new freedom that
came with motoring.*

For the invention of the motor car we can thank a Frenchman, one Nicolas Joseph Cugnot, who in 1769 invented the very first self-propelled road vehicle. This initial effort was steam-powered, and unfortunately not a resounding success; but it was the germ of an idea that evolved through several incarnations into the modern, petrol-powered automobile. The first of these were produced in Germany in the 1880s by Gottlieb Daimler and Karl Benz, and by the end of the century car manufacture had become a thriving industry.

Of course, these really were dream vehicles – sleek, elegant, individual and affordable only by the very rich (until Henry Ford invented the assembly line and reduced production costs). In Britain, the dream car was the child of a highly unlikely marriage of minds in 1904 between Charles Stewart Rolls, an aristocratic car salesman, and Frederick Henry Royce, a self-taught car designer and manufacturer from an impoverished background. Their first creation, the Rolls Royce Silver Ghost, was acclaimed the best in the world; it ran so smoothly that *Autocar* magazine of 20 April 1907 poetically described the feeling as 'one of being wafted through the landscape'. The beautiful mascot, the 'Spirit of Ecstasy', embodies the style and romance of the early motor car.

dream destinations

THE NEW DREAM TRAVELLERS WERE NOW ARRIVING AT THEIR DESTINATION BY ONE OF THE VERY LATEST METHODS OF TRANSPORT — BUT WHO WERE THEY, AND WHAT WAS THEIR PURPOSE IN TRAVELLING?

Travellers of the late 19th and early 20th century fell into two groups. One group was the forerunner of the modern 'package tourist', making an occasional visit here and there, usually under the caring guidance of Thomas Cook; the other was made up of the descendants of the original Grand Tourists, and these were the wealthy aristocrats or would-be upper classes who were following the social 'season', visiting families of similar standing in other countries or hoping to meet a few influential people whose acquaintance would give them a boost up the social ladder. And, of course, there were those parents with daughters of a certain age who were always on the look-out for a suitable husband!

It was perfectly possible to stay in Britain for the whole year, going from one house party to another, but it was far more sophisticated to visit stylish Paris and St Petersburg, cosmopolitan Vienna and Rome, the now glitzy Côte d'Azur and the newly emerging treasure-trove of Egypt.

The Pont de l'Europe, Gare Saint-Lazare, Paris, *painted by Monet in 1877. Windswept passengers (above) look out to sea in a 1923 magazine advertisement.*

A shady adventure for
The Englishman at the
Moulin Rouge, by
Toulouse-Lautrec, 1892.

Les Grands Boulevards,
painted by Renoir in
1875. The Eiffel Tower
(right), painted by
Seurat in 1889, the
year it was built.

Paris at the turn of the 19th century bore little resemblance to the city visited on the Grand Tour. Gone were the narrow streets with gutters that splashed mud (and worse) at the unwary passer-by; now there were wide, elegant boulevards, large shops, the Eiffel Tower. The treasures of Versailles were lost in the French Revolution, but new collections filled the Louvre's Great Gallery. Between 1855 and 1900, Paris hosted five world fairs, each spawning a wave of building – smart hotels to charm the wealthy into spending their money on all that was fresh and chic.

Paris now led the world in gastronomy, and the Paris season (mercifully short) revolved around endless lunches, teas and dinners, punctuated by drives in the Bois de Boulogne. In the evening there were balls or theatres to attend, and always the hope of finding oneself in the company of dazzling foreign aristocrats.

And of course there was the irresistibly shady side of Paris – Montmartre, where Toulouse-Lautrec painted the characters of the demi-monde, and other artists, musicians and writers starved in garrets for the sake of their art. Where else but Paris could a life of destitution take on such a wonderfully romantic air?

An 1897 poster by Mucha advertising trains for Monte Carlo. A couple (below) dance the curious turkey trot.

A 1938 poster for the Côte d'Azur – 'Land of your Dreams'.

The Mediterranean Côte d'Azur, too, had seen an amazing transformation since the days of the 18th-century Grand Tour. No longer was it the seedy and dangerous haunt of pirates and bandits; now it was the place to go to escape the chill of mid-winter.

Monte Carlo, in the tiny principality of Monaco, had become a gamblers' paradise, its famous new casino attracting the wealthy and often reducing them rapidly to poverty. The town was once described as 'a glamorous place where money lost its normal value'; regrettably, there were frequent suicides when the normal value re-asserted itself and the realization of financial ruin set in.

In time, casinos were opened all along the coast, in places with names that still have the power to bewitch with their singularly racy edge – Nice, Cannes, Beaulieu and Menton. Luxurious trains converged on the coast from as far away as Calais and St Petersburg. The journey aimed to put travellers in a frivolous mood; there were card-tables on board, and from the late 1920s the enticingly named Côte d'Azur Pullman provided a carriage reserved specially for dancing the new-fangled American turkey trot and Charleston (attired in full evening dress, naturally).

MONACO·MONTE-CARLO

*Magic and mystery –
characters at one of the
famous Venice carnivals,
depicted in 1919
by Brunelleschi.*

*A poster advertising
rail travel to the
International Exhibition
held in Rome in 1911.*

Italy was still valued for its cultural heritage, but here too there was a social element thrown in that made it great fun for visitors.

Life in Milan continued to revolve around the Opera, which was a marvellous opportunity for going out dressed up beautifully, listening to some of the world's most stunning music in an auditorium with perfect acoustics, then having a late supper. Part of the delight lay in eavesdropping on the composers, artistes and impresarios, who gathered together and hotly debated all aspects of the performance.

Venice was no longer a powerful commercial centre, but had become an exciting resort with parties in the grand palaces, now mostly owned by rich foreigners, and a generous sprinkling of intellectuals. Florence retained its traditional role as a magnet for art lovers, but Rome, in addition to its whole collection of fascinating, newly unearthed ancient monuments, had acquired a monarchy with the unification of Italy under the House of Savoy in 1870, and with it a new social scene of glittering balls and entertainments.

Rome's gain was Naples' loss, though, and with the end of Bourbon rule the once glamorous city degenerated rapidly. However, Vesuvius held its appeal and the ever-resourceful Thomas Cook provided a funicular train for visitors.

Vienna at play, with the huge ferris wheel in the Reisenrad Fairground in the background.

A court ball at the Hofburg Palace, Vienna, painted in 1900 by Wilhelm Gause.

Vienna, in what was then Austria-Hungary, was a fabulous place to visit in the late 19th and early 20th centuries, and all the better if you arrived in style on the *Orient Express*. It was cultural, it was intellectual and it was fun.

The city had come into its own with the creation in the 1860s of the Ringstrasse, a boulevard dotted with all the important buildings from the university to the museums. At the heart of the high life was the Court Opera, home of the still-famous Vienna Philharmonic. Here, the city's much-loved composer Johann Strauss conducted his elegant music at the annual ball, and the aristocracy engaged in their favourite pastime – the floaty, revolving Viennese waltz.

The excesses of frivolity could be tempered by visits to the art and natural history museums or the palaces of the ruling Hapsburgs and other grand families. The city's countless coffee houses were a must for thinkers and intellectuals or those who at least wanted to rub shoulders with the intelligentsia, for this is where the new 'modern' artists, musicians and psychologists gathered.

And when a breath of fresh air was called for, there were trips to the surrounding woodland, immortalized by Strauss in his *Tales from the Vienna Woods* (predictably, a waltz!).

St Petersburg in the last heady days of Imperial Russia – the classical building is the Imperial Bank.

A poster advertising the CIWL service from London to St Petersburg; in winter, journeys were completed in a carriage drawn on sledges (right).

Had the St Petersburg of imperial Russia been easily accessible to the culture-seekers of the 18th century, the Grand Tour would have needed an extra year or two to complete. As it was, there were just a few golden years when trains ran from Paris to Peter the Great's impressive imperial capital before the socialist revolution in 1917 saw the violent end of the tsarist reign.

The city came into being in 1703 and was built by European architects – hence the baroque style. Peter the Great's daughter, Elizabeth, added the Winter Palace, and Catherine the Great the magnificent Hermitage.

Strangely for a city that basked in the midnight sun at the height of summer, the St Petersburg 'season' was in the dark of mid-winter – very romantic, if you could stand the cold. The city was vibrant and exciting, with luxurious hotels and restaurants, fabulous shopping, theatres and concerts, the wonderful ballet for which Russia is so famous, and haunting gypsy music. There were street entertainers, toboggan runs and sled rides pulled by reindeer on the frozen Neva river. And for a privileged few, there was the hospitality of influential, and soon to be exiled, families such as the Stroganoffs and Orlovs.

The Sphinx at Giza, painted by David Roberts when only its head was visible above the sand.

English tourists enjoy a camel-back ride, from W.H. Russell's A Diary in the East, 1869.

Winter-sun seekers who preferred culture to the Côte d'Azur casinos headed for Egypt, a magical land whose treasures were slowly coming to light at the end of the 19th century.

From the port of Alexandria, travellers took a train to Cairo, where the markets were enchanting and the nearby Pyramids of Giza and the Sphinx enthralling. A visit to the new Egyptian Museum was a must, for here the mysteries of the ancient civilization were revealed. Later travellers could admire the treasure of Tutankhamen, the 'Boy King', whose magnificent tomb at Thebes was unearthed in 1922 by the English Egyptologist Howard Carter and his patron, Lord Carnarvon.

A tantalizingly uneasy frisson surrounded the discovery, as the disturbance of the tomb was said to have released the legendary curse of the pharaohs and caused Carnarvon's death the following year.

The scene set, the journey continued to its dazzling finale, a trip up the Nile. Those of a romantic disposition travelled under sail by dahabiah; others preferred the unabashed comfort of Thomas Cook's paddle steamers. The river banks were lined with endless monuments to the country's history, and the memory of the pharaohs and queens, gods and goddesses of legend – Akhenaten, Amenhotep, Ramses, Nefertiti, Osiris and Hathor – hung in the air above the timeless Egyptian landscape.

The famous French liner Normandie *approaches the port of New York in this illustration of 1937.*

Stylish fashion of the 1920s, set against a background of New York skyscrapers in silhouette.

New York, once only notable as the emigrants' route into the United States, shot to fame as a destination for the bright young things of the 1920s. Europe had momentarily lost its charm beneath the dark cloud of the Great War and its aftermath; in America, on the other hand, business was booming and the new affluence was very much in evidence. It was, quite simply, a more comfortable place to be – at least, until the Wall Street Crash in 1929 saw the end of the fun-filled Roaring Twenties and the start of the Great Depression as economic ruin hit thousands of investors.

Virtually all visitors arrived by one of the huge ocean liners, and headed for the new hotels that sprang up like skybound temples to hedonism. The city was bustling and exciting, with plenty to entertain. By day, there were endless shops and restaurants in which to idle away a few hours; in the evening, there was music, dancing, the theatre ….

Broadway, known as 'the Great White Way' because of its myriad electric signs and billboards, was already the heart of New York's theatreland and the decade saw a new wave of venues. A visitor described the effect of the lights as 'a glowing summer afternoon all night'. Jazz and blues singers such as Duke Ellington and Louis Armstrong converged on the city with their new musical genre; and sedate old-time dancing gave way to the Charleston and 'flappers', liberated young women with short dresses and bobbed hair who flapped and stomped with gay abandon.

A lady golfer enjoys fresh air and exercise as part of her 'cure' at Vichy.

The gastronomic excesses associated with luxury travel led to an occasional need to rest the overtaxed digestive system and lose a few pounds. However, this didn't mean opting out of the social scene – indeed, it was very fashionable to visit a spa and curb one's tendencies to plumpness in the company of the smart set.

In England, 'taking the waters' had become the thing to do during the reign of the Georgians, and particularly the Prince Regent. All the architectural and cultural delights of Bath came into being because of the natural mineral water, which tastes very unpleasant but is said to be very efficacious. Alternatively, one could literally take to the waters by swimming in the sea, preferably in Brighton, another haunt of the prince.

Those who wished to stay abroad for their mid-summer 'cure' had several options – Baden-Baden, Evian, Vittel, Vichy and Karlsbad, among others. The spas were dream destinations with a twist. They had all the grand hotels and restaurants that one could wish for, in the most beautiful surroundings, so that those who spent their days in the healing waters of the thermal springs could then be cured of the cure in their habitual state of extreme luxury!

to see and be seen

GENTLEMEN ON THE 18TH-CENTURY GRAND TOUR OFTEN STAYED IN A CITY FOR SO LONG THAT THEY TOOK LODGINGS IN A HOUSE FOR THE DURATION OF THEIR VISIT. TOURISTS IN THE LATE 19TH AND EARLY 20TH CENTURIES, ON THE OTHER HAND, FLITTED FROM PLACE TO PLACE LIKE MIGRATING BIRDS AS THEY FOLLOWED THE SOCIAL 'SEASON'. SUMPTUOUS TRAINS AND SHIPS BORE THEM TO THEIR DESTINATIONS AND, ONCE THERE, THEY TOOK UP RESIDENCE IN EQUALLY LAVISH HOTELS.

'Anyone for tennis?' at the Heliopolis Palace Hotel, Cairo, c.1930. A menu (above) from The Ritz hotel restaurant – a gastronomic dream.

The concept of the 'grand hotel' came from America, where the world's first luxury hotel opened in Boston in 1829. Soon, opulent hotels were being built in Europe, near railway stations for those journeying on the new trains, in cities where great world exhibitions were held, or simply to accommodate the idle rich whose aim was to see and be seen in all the right places. And there was now such wonderful scope for this!

Some of the best-known luxury hotels of today were built during this era, and in them fragments of the golden age of travelling remain like wistful strains of music – the name of Auguste Escoffier, the great French hotel chef; the mouthwatering Sacher-Torte, served in Vienna's Sacher Hotel; and the magical memory of that outstandingly gifted hotelier, César Ritz.

Winter outside but warmth and elegance within, in this charming illustration of the London Ritz Hotel's Palm Court.

A stylized publicity poster of 1921 for the Hotel Ritz in Paris.

César Ritz – 'the king of hoteliers and hotelier to kings' – will for ever be associated with the grandest of grand hotels. Like Thomas Cook, he burst onto the travel scene from unlikely origins, working his way up through the hotel trade from odd-job man to manager, and eventually to owner. This was a man with a remarkable gift for making people very, very comfortable.

Ritz was born in a Swiss mountain village, so it is highly appropriate that his first success was in Switzerland, where he transformed the Grand Hôtel National in Lucerne from an architecturally impressive but otherwise rather uninviting establishment into a highly desirable one. Switzerland's natural charms were greatly enhanced by the existence of a grand hotel with excellent service, gourmet cooking, stylish entertainment and a generous helping of celebrated guests.

Ritz worked his magic on many other hotels in Europe – the Grand Hotels in Monte Carlo and Rome, to name but two – and gave his name as well as his style to the Paris and London Ritz Hotels. The glamour synonymous with Ritz's hotels inspired the jolly Irving Berlin song *Putting on the Ritz* (which means to get dressed up and do something stylish!).

Fashions for summer on the Hotel Excelsior Beach at the Lido in Venice, 1929. The Grand Hotel in Rome (above), an illustration from the Great Hotels of the World series by Philip Le Bas.

Monsieur Ritz set the standard for European grand hotels, which sprang up in every city frequented by the well-heeled traveller. The various Paris exhibitions saw the building of the Grand Hôtel du Louvre, the Hôtel Continental and the Hôtel du Quai d'Orsay; the Hotel Meurice was favoured for its elegant rooftop dining.

In Vienna, the cognoscenti headed for Sacher's, behind the Court Opera, famous for the Sacher-Torte, a delectable chocolate cake, and for some deliciously dangerous liaisons; in St Petersburg, the best hotels were the Astoria and the Hotel de l'Europe, to which the winter visitor was transported from the station, snugly wrapped in furs for warmth, in a droshky, a low, horse-drawn open carriage on steel runners.

In Venice, where bathing in the Lido had become the summer craze, the Hotel Excelsior was much loved for its great style and its beach frontage. Rome's Grand Hotel was given the 'Ritz' treatment so that royal visitors to the new Italian monarchy had somewhere to stay that was worthy of their status and their high expectations. Needless to say, the Grand was a great success and earned Ritz the witty nickname of 'the new César'.

Home of style and a classic salad, the Waldorf-Astoria Hotel, New York, in 1896.

Shepheard's Hotel, Cairo, in 1905 (below right), and its luggage label (right) showing the Pyramids and the Sphinx at Giza.

CAIRO
EGYPT

SHEPHEARD'S
HOTEL

Further afield, in Egypt's capital, Cairo, was an hotel that was nothing short of an institution. Shepheard's was a European stronghold with intriguing antecedents, having been converted from a harem; under the ownership of Thomas Cook, it was so popular that it had to be extended several times. A verandah faced onto the boulevard on which the hotel stood, so that guests could relax at rattan tables and watch the bustling world go by, while at the rear was a large, peaceful garden. Shepheard's met a sad and sudden end when it was burned down by nationalists in 1952.

Wealthy visitors to a completely different kind of city, New York, headed for hotels built by the Astors, a shrewd business family made great by the enterprising son of a butcher from Waldorf in Germany (hence the famous hotel name, the Waldorf-Astoria). If the delicious Waldorf Salad isn't enough to keep this name in mind, then the Broadway hotel's frequent appearance in films and books certainly will. The Astors' first endeavour, Astor House, pioneered the luxury of hot-water plumbing – an innovation for which subsequent travellers to European copies of the American grand hotel must have been extremely grateful!

all dressed up

A luggage label for the Hotel Touring at Milan in Italy. A 1920s fashion plate (above) illustrates what to wear to enjoy the romance of rail travel to the full!

IN THE GOLDEN AGE OF TRAVEL, THE WELL-TO-DO TRAVELLER KNEW HOW TO DO THINGS IN STYLE. TAKING A TRIP WASN'T SIMPLY A MATTER OF THROWING A FEW THINGS INTO A SUITCASE (EVER MINDFUL OF BAGGAGE WEIGHT RESTRICTIONS), DONNING A PAIR OF JEANS AND A T-SHIRT AND HEADING FOR THE AIRPORT; EVERYTHING WAS DONE WITH GRACE AND ELEGANCE.

Luggage was an art form in itself – trunks of all sizes, hat boxes, dressing cases, all in beautifully tooled, hard-wearing leather – and there was an endless supply of smartly liveried porters at every railway station, port and hotel to carry it. Displaying the distinctive luggage labels of the smartest establishments was a subtle way of drawing attention to your wealth and good taste.

Clothes to wear on the journey took careful consideration, for even a relatively short journey on a luxury train involved appropriate changes of dress, and long sea-crossings and cruises called for an entire wardrobe. And what you didn't take with you, you bought when you reached your destination, for shopping had taken on a new dimension.

The acquisition of souvenirs had changed, too, and the 18th-century Grand Tour passion for sombre classical collections to adorn the home had given way to a far more eclectic taste.

In the 1920s a girl could be generous with her luggage, knowing that a discreet railway porter would take care of it.

'If in doubt, take everything with you' seems to be the motto of this young traveller.

Matching 'designer luggage' was de rigueur for the affluent traveller – would they choose Vuitton or Asprey to supply their needs? Quality was as important as style, as the traveller who followed the social season could easily visit half a dozen countries in one year, and luggage that could stand the constant embarking and disembarking of trains was essential.

Luggage came in all shapes and sizes. One of the most useful pieces was a huge, hinged trunk that, when stood on end and opened up, revealed itself to be a sort of mobile armoire, with a stack of drawers on one side and a hanging rail on the other; smaller cases took care of things that could be safely transported flat. Hat boxes were a must, for no self-respecting lady would dream of venturing out without a hat to match her outfit, and to have one's favourite millinery confection squashed would have been unthinkable.

For gentlemen travellers, a good dressing case was necessary to transport shaving gear – a silver razor, badger-hair shaving brush, crystal bottle of bay rum cologne and so forth; and ladies needed a secure case to store precious jewels, away from prying eyes and light fingers.

These 1920s outfits for driving are aptly named 'Cherchez la Femme'.

This evening gown, illustrated in the Gazette du Bon Ton in 1925, was designed by the couturier Worth.

Dressing for the occasion was one of the chief delights of luxury travel, but could also be one of the tribulations. Followers of the season were faced with endless social scenarios, each of which required a different set of clothes. Obviously, gowns were needed for both day and evening wear, but it was also necessary to plan for the possibilities of being invited to ride, hunt, skate, bathe, play tennis, go motoring or cycling ….

Eventually, it was possible to go into a shop and buy something suitable 'off the peg'; originally, however, every item of clothing was made by a tailor for the gentlemen or dressmaker for the ladies. Most ladies had their entire wardrobe made for them before setting off on their travels, but the exceptionally wealthy made sure their itinerary included a visit to Paris to be dressed by one of the famous couturiers – the new name for a dressmaker.

It must have come as something of a relief for the female traveller when the fashion for long, flared skirts and hooped gowns gave way to the shorter, sleeker lines of the post-Great War years. Laws of etiquette were relaxed a little and ladies were able to put comfort and convenience above the cumbersome restraints of feminine modesty.

*A clock from the
workshop of Fabergé in
St Petersburg. A tourist
haggles in the dark and
mysterious depths of a
Cairo bazaar (right).*

While Britain led the way for travelling, Paris led the way for shopping. All the delights on display at the world fairs found their way into the city's new department stores – Au Printemps, La Samaritaine, Bon Marché; here one could buy the latest designs in crystal, silver and porcelain, a different kind of souvenir to enchant visitors. Other cities were quick to follow suit and shopping became the new pastime. In New York, Macy's grew into a Broadway department store from a number of smaller shops, and Bloomingdale's East Side Bazaar was selling European goods by 1872.

St Petersburg, the Russian equivalent of Paris for style and fashion, had specialities of its own on its main boulevard, Nevsky. There were foreign bookstores, a wonderful art-nouveau delicatessen selling gourmet foods such as caviar, and of course the famous jeweller Fabergé. It also had an oriental-type souk, selling all sorts of exotic goods; dream travellers headed for the real thing in Cairo, with its stalls of precious carpets, spices, scarabs (mostly imitation) and antiquities (also mostly imitation) set amid a noisy, exciting, constantly moving sea of street urchins, snake-charmers and whirling dervishes.

LVNDI AVX 3 MARS

GALERIES LAFAYETTE

MAISON VENDANT LE MEILLEUR MARCHÉ DE TOUT PARIS

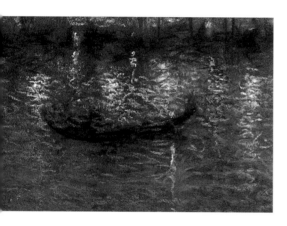

Details from Fireworks over Venice *(above and right), a flamboyant illustration in pastels by Lucien Levy-Dhurmer.*

So are those days of dream travel gone for ever? At first sight, it seems that the answer is a resounding 'yes'.

But if we choose carefully, we can go back. We can board the *Orient Express* and journey overnight to Venice in opulent style. We can listen to Strauss's waltzes at the atmospheric New Year's Day concert in Vienna and imagine ourselves part of the colourful, swirling tide of elegantly attired dancers at the annual Court Ball. We can take a suite at the Paris Ritz and feel the ghostly caress of César as he lovingly tends to our every whim. We can take a leisurely voyage across the Atlantic on the Cunard Line's luxurious new ship, *Queen Mary 2*, or cruise up the Nile in the wake of Thomas Cook's enchanted tourists of a hundred years ago.

We may have to do all this in bite-sized pieces, for few of us are able to drift lazily from one place to another for several months, or even weeks. But perhaps in our frenetic, 21st-century lives, this is the best way to do it – to awaken from one glorious dream and know that a lovely new dream is already waiting to be discovered.

acknowlededgments

Photographs are reproduced by kind permission of the following:

Bridgeman Art Library: Front cover, pp1, 3 (Archives Charmet), 8 (Private Collection), 8 background/ 9 (Monastery of La Rabida, Huelva, Andalusia), 10 (Private Collection), 11 (Victoria and Albert Museum), 18 (Rafael Valls Gallery, London), 18 background/19 (Private Collection), 20 (Musée des Beaux-Arts, Rouen), 21 (Chateau du Grand Trianon, Versailles), 22 (Agnew & Sons, London), 23 (Bibliotheque de L'Opera, Paris), 24 (Private Collection), 25 (Collection of the Earl of Leicester, Holkham Hall, Norfolk), 26 (Sir John Soane's Museum, London), 27 (Yale Center for British Art, Paul Mellon Collection, USA/photo: Bridgeman), 28 right (Victoria and Albert Museum), 29 (Christie's Images), 30 (Private Collection), 31 (Musée Marmottan, Paris), 32 right (Bibliotheque des Arts Decoratifs, Paris), 33 (Archives Charmet), 35 (Archives Charmet), 42 (Herbert Art Gallery and Museum, Coventry), 43 (Christopher Wood Gallery, London), 45 (Musée Marmottan, Paris), 46 left (Private Collection), 46 right (Fine Arts Museum of San Francisco), 47 (Musée Toulouse-Lautrec, Albi), 48 left (Archives Charmet), 49 (Mucha Trust), 50 (Collection Kharbine-Tapabor, Paris), 52 (Historisches Museum der Stadt, Vienna), 53 (The Fine Art Society, London), 54 left (Archives Charmet), 54 right (Private Collection), 55 (Bibliotheque Nationale, Paris), 57 (The Stapleton Collection), 58 (Archives Charmet), 61 (Archives Charmet), 62 (Archives Charmet), 64 (Index/BAL), 65 (Private Collection), 66 (Archives Charmet), 67 (Portal Gallery Ltd), 69 (Museum of the City of New York), 70/70 background (Private Collection), 72 (Private Collection), 74 (Archives Charmet), 75 (Archives Charmet), 76 left (Private Collection), 77 (Archives Charmet), 78, 79 and back cover (Peter Willi).

Jarrold Publishing (courtesy of Newby Hall, Yorkshire): p28 (left).

Mary Evans Picture Library: pp6, 14, 15, 16, 17, 30 background, 34 left, 34 right, 36, 37, 38, 39, 41, 44/44 background, 48 right (by Steve Rumney), 51, 56, 59, 60, 62 background/63, 68 left, 68 right, 71, 73, 76 right.

Science & Society Picture Library: pp12, 13, 32 left, 40 left, 40 right.

Victoria & Albert Museum: p7.

Luggage label motif by Mark Buckingham.